Verena Schuster

Short Stories for Moms

Energizing and Inspiring 10-Minute Reads for the Soul

To my parents, who taught me to live with altruism, strength, and humility, showed me the necessary boundaries, and gave me unconditional love.

– Thank you!

Content

About the Author

Verena Schuster was born in 1991 in Geesthacht but has since settled in the district of Lüneburg. After leaving school, she trained as a vocal coach and later as a kindergarten teacher. It became clear to her early on that she wanted to put her personal experiences into writing to be published. Since 2020, she has been working as an author, creating literary works by commission. She always writes with passion, sensitivity, and humor.

Living with her large family to this day, she is intimately familiar with family life in all its aspects. Above all, she appreciates the individuality of all her family members and the solidarity she experiences anew every day.

In the book "Short Stories for Moms," she explores a mother's life from various perspectives. It's important to her to acknowledge and take seriously the challenges of motherhood while taking them on in a humorous and refreshing way. In an ironic yet sensitive way, she pays tribute to the everyday heroines, offers new perspectives, and gives both new and experienced moms a few moments of relaxation and escape during the day.

Our Everyday Heroines

Congratulations – you're an everyday heroine! You may have only recently been confronted with this important task or already weathered through the defiant phase, the time of self-discovery and your child's puberty.

Whether these times are still ahead of you or already behind you is irrelevant because one thing always remains the same: a mother goes through the ups and downs with her child, sharing laughter and tears, arguments, and making up time and time again. In these short stories, you'll get to know moms who are just like any other. They make mistakes, have unusual ideas, stumble over hurdles, and get back up. They're confronted with the pitfalls of everyday life and learn how to deal with them.

A mother often has less time for herself than she would like. With these short stories, you'll experience 30 little time-outs in your everyday life as a mom. Deliberately kept short, they read quickly and smoothly, blending emotion and humor. With wit and charm, you're bound to recognize yourself in one or two stories. Hopefully, you'll laugh and gain a new perspective on yourself.

As a mom, you're often first and foremost there for your child, worrying out of your mind and letting your nerves get the better of you. But what would these hurdles be without the love, unity, and moments of happiness that always accompany your life together?

Ten minutes out of your day - sources of energy that'll provide you with renewed strength and fresh ideas; these are all short stories for moms. They're written for you!

To our everyday heroines, to family, to love!

1. Full Body Portrait

Amelie turns to the right and left, lifting her top to examine the skin that had so beautifully stretched around her belly button just a few months ago. With her top lifted, she turns to the right and left for another look.

"Well?" her husband chimes in with a grin, and she quickly pulls down her top. But it's too late. "Have we been dancing again?" Amelie feels herself blushing. When her husband stands next to her in the full-length mirror, he lifts his shirt and spins around several times, shaking his butt; she teasingly elbows him in the side. She'd never been willing to admit how much the change in her body had bothered her. The radiant baby glow she'd had at the beginning of the pregnancy was long gone. And even though she could finally see her feet again, she still couldn't shake that lingering discomfort in her own skin.

"Seriously," Ben says, pulling his shirt down. "You have to stop hanging around in front of the mirror. You've been standing in front of it, looking at yourself for at least five minutes every day since Emmy was born. If I didn't know better, I'd say you preferred your body to mine." Amelie puts her hands on her hips and opens her mouth, but Ben doesn't let her get a word in edgeways. "Two and a half hours," he says. "Emmy is 30 days old now. If we add up the five minutes a day you are looking in that mirror, that equals two and a half hours." As Ben leaves the room, she hears his last snarky comment from the hallway. "The things we could have done in two and a half hours."

Amelie collapses onto the bed. This was, precisely, her problem. She'd never allow Ben to see what her body looks like right now. Her stomach sags, decorated with stretch-marks, and her breasts seem disproportionately large compared to the rest of her body.

Amelie gazes at herself, sitting down in the mirror. But this time, she focuses on her face. She looks tired, notices the wrinkles around her eyes, and feels like she's aged more than she expected since becoming pregnant. Amelie studies herself for a while when she finally hears Ben calling from the bottom of the stairs, "Dinner's ready." Sighing, she gets up and heads downstairs.

The delicious aroma of spaghetti carbonara fills the air, a dish no one can cook as wonderfully as her husband. And yet today, she puts her fork down well before the feeling of fullness kicks in. Ben raises an eyebrow skeptically, pro-vocatively shovels several overflowing forks of spaghetti into his mouth, savors every bite, swallows, and holds out a full fork to his wife.

As she turns it down, Ben puts down his fork. "Don't you have any idea how beautiful you are?" he says, walking around the table to sit directly next to Amelie. She opens her mouth to object, but Ben again refuses to let her get a word in. He gently brushes his fingers around her eyes, tracing the delicate lines developed over the past few months. "These lines are laugh lines. They appeared when we found out we were going to be parents. They represent the moment when we first heard Emmy's heartbeat. They deepened when we learned we were expecting a girl."

Ben's hands move to Amelie's belly. "Our baby grew in this belly. The skin around it stretched to give our girl the space she needed. It'll gradually regain some of its shape, but now it's proof that your body was our baby's home until recently." Ben lifts Amelie's shirt slightly and runs his thumb over the scar. "Through this scar, our baby was brought into the world. It'll remind us of all our lives from the day we met our baby for the first time. This scar describes the most beautiful moment we have ever experienced and ever will." Ben cradles Amelie's face. "You look different than a few months ago. But in my eyes, you've never been more beautiful than you are now. A few months ago, you were my wife. Today, you're so much more than that. You're my wife and the mother of my baby. And that's who I want to see every day!"

When Ben offers Amelie the fork again, she takes a bite. And as she hears the soft cries of her baby through the baby monitor, she feels her smile deepening the tiny wrinkles around her eyes ever so slightly – and that was perfectly fine!

2. The Grumpy Monster

"My dearest Lily, please be so kind as to come out of the bathroom and get ready for school."

"Hey, Lily, come on, get out of that bathroom. It's time to head to school."

"Lily, make sure you get ready. School's starting soon."

Tatjana tries out various sentences in her head before knocking on the bathroom door. But in the end, she doesn't need to use any of them.

A drawn-out "Uuuuuuuhhhhh" from her daughter penetrates through the door. And if Tatjana isn't mistaken, her daughter mumbles a grumpy "Leave me alone" just after it.

"Lily, breakfast is ready, and school is about to start. Please come down," Tatjana shouts through the door in a friendly tone. She hears the key turning loudly in the lock. And, as always, when she hasn't seen her daughter in the morning, she expects a grumpy monster to soon come running towards her. A shaggy, hairy monster with eyes perpetually rolled in annoyance, ears overflowing with cotton wool so it doesn't hear anything, and a mouth sewn shut in a thin line. After all, her daughter has recently developed into such a grumpy monster.

But like every morning, Tatjana looks at her now fourteen-year-old daughter in amazement as she finally appears in front of her. "Why are you staring at me like that?" Lily asks. But Tatjana just shakes her head in bewilderment. Instead of a tousled monster with a distorted face, the young girl she knows so well stands right there. Only subtle lipstick, mascara, and thin eyeliner have been added.

"You look very pretty," Tatjana says with complete sincerity. Even though her daughter has transformed into a typical teenager during puberty, she hides it behind a beautiful face. "Mom, you're embarrassing," says the grumpy monster lurking inside her daughter. But as Lily heads downstairs, Tatjana sees the smile spreading across Lily's face.

"Want some?" Lily's father holds out a roll to the teenager, but she brushes him off. "Dad, honestly," she says, filling a bowl with cereal and fruit.

"Dad, honestly," Tatjana chides her husband with a wink. "You know grumpy monsters would never shovel empty calories into their bodies." Lily nods at her mom. "At least you get it," she says and silently spoons the cereal into her mouth.

"I wanted to talk to you again about the party," says Tatjana, broaching the delicate subject that she, her husband, and the grumpy monster have been tiptoeing for several days. Lily puts her spoon down anxiously. "What's left to discuss? You guys are old and uncool and don't want me to have fun." This time, Tatjana looks sternly at her daughter. "It was funny until now," she says seriously. "But you've just crossed a line."

"Sorry," Lily murmurs softly. Tatjana nods. It's reassuring to know that beneath what has come over Lily, her daughter is still there.

"Dad and I talked again. We think we forbid you from going to the party too quickly." Lily's eyes light up because THE PARTY is, after all, what her class has been talking about for weeks. It's supposed to be at a classmate's house, and his parents won't be home.

"You know Dad and I worry about you," Tatjana explains. "A party without parents can quickly get out of control. That's why we want to establish some rules that we'll discuss beforehand. This is your chance to prove to us that we can still trust you despite the grumpy monster. Are you okay with that?"

In a burst of excitement, Lily jumps into her mom's arms. "Lily!" Tatjana exclaims, disgusted. "Don't do that. You're embarrassing!" Giving her mom the evils, Lily grabs her school bag and leaves, muttering quietly, "Mom, seriously!" And Tatjana watches her grumpy monster go, knowing that her daughter is protected by that thick monster's skin.

3. Alien Mom

With her left arm, Maria reaches for the kettle. Meanwhile, her right hand is occupied with crumbling the baby's biscuit. Maria's right hand is in charge of mashing the banana, while her left foot keeps the baby entertained. Using the arm growing from her left temple, she packs the nappies and changing pad into the bag. The arm sprouting from her right shoulder doubles in size to search for the baby's pacifier. Maria sings a nursery rhyme to the baby with one mouth while the other reminds her husband to fill up the car with petrol. Maria maintains her balance on the leg that grew after giving birth, as her other legs were occupied with more pressing matters. With one ear, the new mom listens to check if her baby is still in a good mood, while the other ear listens for her friend ringing the doorbell. Her third ear tries to determine whether it's going stay dry today, as the picnic planned by Maria, her husband, and a couple they're friends with can't fall through.

"The bell rang; can you please open the door?" Maria calls to her husband while her second mouth transitions to mimicking different animal sounds for the baby. But the ear, which has grown specifically for her husband, can't hear a response. With a powerful swing, Maria extends her arm from the right shoulder even further, trying to navigate it through the hallway to push down the door handle. "I'll be right there," she calls to her friend who enters the house – holding her baby in one arm, her husband's hand with the other, and the baby's bag with the third. With her fourth hand, she hugs Maria, reaching forward with her upper body because all four arms are occupied. Finally, the baby biscuit is dissolved in boiled water, mixed with banana puree, and stored in a small tupperware. The dummies have been found, and the nappies are packed in the baby bag. When Maria's husband comes in, she thanks him for filling up the car. The baby is still giggling quietly, allowing Maria to momentarily stop singing through her "entertainer mouth." The ear tuned in to the weather report also gives the all-clear, so she can rest that briefly.

"Shall we?" she asks her husband and the couple, full of anticipation. Together, they load the packed baby and picnic bags into the boot, put the babies in their car seats, and jump in the car. As the little ones fall asleep to the monotonous sound of the engine, Maria doesn't know what to do with her second mouth, which is usually busy entertaining. Her third hand feels rather obsolete as well. Not using her fourth hand feels so wrong that Maria cautiously checks the seat to see if there's a lost cuddly toy under there. Her three legs tap on the floor in a complicated rhythm –

otherwise, the mom would feel seriously under-challenged. Only her ears are fully occupied as they simultaneously listen to her friend's stories and the men's banter while keeping an ear out for any sign of the babies waking up. But that's okay because Maria's friend is also fidgeting with as many limbs as her. After all, they're not used to so much peace and quiet.

Who doesn't know these kinds of moms with many legs, ears, mouths, arms, and hands? What would they do if they had to manage with just two arms, legs, ears, and a mouth? Fortunately, in an emergency, a mom can split herself up to be in multiple places at once – but it's rare to see because moms are able to manage without. These powers are passed to every mom once the baby arrives. But seriously, imagine if she couldn't do all that, she'd almost be super-human!

4. A Pinch of Spice

"We would like you to come along with your son for a discussion on 3rd April at 12:00." Anneliese reads the note that Erik passed to her, who is now sitting across the table looking down at the floor. "Is this from Mrs. Dorn?" Anneliese asks, and her son nods sadly. Anneliese narrows her eyes. Of course, she knows it's not a good sign when the principal, Mrs. Dorn, summons them both for a chat. Working at the local elementary school, Anneliese is quite familiar with the principal. She knows the principal only calls parents when their children get into trouble.

"Do you want to tell me what this is all about?" she asks her son. Erik looks down, mumbling something under his breath. Anneliese stands up and sits next to her him. "You know you can trust me, right?"

She interrupts his quiet mumbling. Eventually, her son looks up and bursts into tears. "I've done something really terrible," he confesses. Anneliese takes a deep breath, hoping desperately that no one has been harmed in the process. Nodding, she listens to her child and then picks up the phone.

"I'd like to speak with the principal," she asks the school secretary a few rings later. Erik looks at his mom inquisitively, but she waves him once she hears Mrs. Dorn's voice on the other line. "I think we can skip the parent-teacher meeting tomorrow," Anneliese gets straight to the point. Erik could hear the principal's soft voice coming through the phone, but he couldn't make out a word. "That's correct," his mom continues. "He told me he's been accused of cheating, but it's all just a silly misunderstanding." Erik frowns. There was definitely no misunderstanding about him taking the German test his mom had prepared for her German class to show his friend Hans. Hans struggled in German and desperately needed a good grade. And because Erik's mom had already prepared the test for her class, he thought he could slip it to his friend during the break so that he could think of the answers in advance. It was just bad luck that he accidentally pulled it out during class, and his math teacher spotted it.

Erik listens as his mom continues, "I bought a new school bag for myself yesterday. You know my back often hurts, so I really needed something more supportive. But the problem is that it looks quite similar to Erik's school bag, and I accidentally put the test paper inside. I want to apologize for this misunderstanding. I'll draft a new exam paper today, so no student has an advantage."

After hanging up the phone, Anneliese looks at her son. "You understand that you made a mistake, don't you?" she asks, and Erik nods timidly. Anneliese takes his hand and says, "You know, there are serious mistakes that hurt other people – physically or emotionally. Those mistakes are serious, and you need to understand what they mean for others. And then there are mistakes like the one you made today." Erik looks up at his mom cautiously. "Silly mistakes?" he asks, and Anneliese smiles at him. "You were trying to help Hans, right?" Erik nods, and Anneliese explains, "You meant well but made the wrong decision. Cheating won't help Hans. What would really help him is if you both studied together. After all, you're learning the same things in class. Maybe there are other ways you can help him. But we'll think about that in the car; I'm in a hurry."

Erik hesitates. "Well," his mom explains, "I've got to prepare a new exam paper for my German class later. But before that, I need to buy a new bag for work, which must look just like yours; otherwise, Mrs. Dirn will immediately clock on to my small lie today. I think we both have a big challenge ahead, don't you think?"

As Anneliese gets into the car, she smiles to herself. Her young boy still has much to learn. But what is much more important is that cheating needs to be learned - and she'll just have to give him a push in the right direction. Because, as everyone knows, a little harmless cheating is like salt in the soup - it works without it, but it only becomes interesting with a pinch of spice.

5. The Walking Mommy

Tina looks around. She's convinced that a largely invisible bell has materialized over her head in the last few days. It muffles every sound as if she's surrounded by cotton wool and blurs her visions as if she's looking through a thick wall of fog. But no matter where she looks, she can't discern the golden, metallic bell under which she feels trapped.

"Hello? Anyone there?" Tina gazes at her husband, Henry, who is now playfully flicking his index finger in front of her eyes. "Sorry?" she stammers, again feeling trapped within her small, tired world. "I asked what we're having for lunch today." Tina needs a moment to remember that "lunch" means she needs to prepare a meal. After all, Henry has an appointment at work. And isn't it the duty of a good mom and homemaker to put food on the table for her husband when he gets home?

While Tina mulls this over, she sees Henry shaking his head. "I think I'll grab something at work," he suggests.

Tina nods gratefully, relieved that the kitchen can be kept cold today. She'll make herself a sandwich later, provided the bell doesn't cloud her vision too much.

"You really need to catch up on some sleep when Danny's napping," Henry advises. He contorts his face and raises his hands like a zombie. "If you keep going like this, you'll turn into 'The Walking Mommy.'" Only after the front door has closed behind Henry does Tina remember that she could have laughed at the joke. "The Walking Mommy," she mutters softly as she fetches Danny, who she can hear waking up in his cot.

As the key turns in the lock, Tina barely registers that the day has flown by. Like the last few days, she has been shuffling around the house, preoccupied with Danny under a bell of tiredness, feeling quite alone and isolated.

A delicate smell of food rises to Tina's nose. It creeps under the edge of the bell directly into her nose. Suddenly, she is aware of the hunger she hasn't felt all day.

"I've brought your favorite," Henry says, waving the chopsticks for the Chinese takeout in front of Tina's nose.

However, unlike what she expected, he doesn't set the table. Instead, he places two candles on the living room table, spreading blankets on the sofa. He gently takes the sleeping baby from Tina's arms and guides her to the couch. Then he hands his wife the food and wraps both of them in the largest living room blanket. Tina looks at her husband with a questioning expression, but he waves it off. "I heard Walking Mommy need their breaks. They need to eat, sleep, and be taken care of. And I thought we've reached the point where you need a little looking after."

Forgetting to chew the bite she had just put up to her mouth, Tina realizes that in recent weeks, she'd been caring for her baby every moment - mornings, afternoons, evenings, and even nights. It hadn't occurred to her that there hadn't been anyone taking care of her for a long time. She couldn't remember the last time she consciously had a warm meal, had a bath in peace, or had a full night's sleep. Instead, she'd been feeding and bathing Danny and ensuring her little baby could sleep peacefully.

Just like that morning, Tina looks around. She can't see the bell but can feel it's still there. However, something has changed. Tonight, under her bell, she no longer feels alone. Tonight, her husband has joined her. And even though the bell won't just simply disappear, having her partner by her side makes it feel much cozier. After finishing her meal, Tina lies down on Henry's legs. She closes her eyes, knowing that Danny is safe and protected in Henry's arms. As she falls asleep, she senses the bell retreat slightly. And who knows – perhaps with a little care, it'll soon be completely gone.

6. Love Grass

"Mommy, look." Lisa hears her daughter's voice but looks at her watch, stressed. Like every morning, the two of them have left far too late. "Mommy, now look." But Lisa has no time. Drop-off time at the kindergarten was almost up, and her boss was certainly not happy when she was late for work. "Nele, we're in a hurry," she says, pulling her daughter behind her. When she realizes that her daughter is starting to run beside her, she picks her up.

"Goodbye, Flowers!" Lisa hears her daughter's soft voice and feels Nele waving at something behind her.

"Goodbye, honey," Lisa says goodbye to her child a few minutes later. She waves to Nele and blows her a big kiss one last time. Then, she walks to catch the bus that'll drop her at work. She barely makes it in time. She can feel her heart racing in her chest. She takes a few deep breaths to shake off the remaining stress that clings to her. The next moment, her gaze is captivated by the colorful sea of flowers in the park. Yellow, red, blue, and purple colors compete to be the most beautiful. These flowers must have been freshly planted the day before because they weren't there yesterday. Lisa keeps the flowers in her sight for as long as possible. When she turns around, she notices that the other passengers on the bus don't seem to notice them. Their eyes are down, either looking at their phones, reading books, or with their eyes closed.

"It's a shame that many adults fail to notice the small, beautiful moments. Everyone, except for me, missed this unique moment of beauty," she thinks when her daughter's voice suddenly echoes in her ears.

"Mommy, look. Mommy, please look. Goodbye, flowers!" And then she realizes that not everyone missed the sight - quite the opposite. Four-year-old Nele noticed the sea of flowers on their way to kindergarten. She'd made such an effort to try and get her mom's attention. But just like the adults on the bus with Lisa at that moment, in the early morning, Lisa had, too, missed it. She was in too much of a rush, preoccupied with the ticking clock, and wasn't paying attention.

When Lisa picks up her daughter from kindergarten that day, she's in for a very special surprise. "For you, Mommy," the little girl says, holding out a green bouquet of spring wildflowers to her mom. "I picked these flowers for you." A girl from Nele's kindergarten group laughs at what Nele calls 'flowers.' "Those aren't flowers," the older girl says knowingly. "It's just grass. The flowers in the park are real flowers, and they are much prettier and much more colorful." Nele's arm, holding the spring grass, droops sadly as the older girl disappears.

"Nonsense," says Lisa and reaches for the little bouquet. She takes her daughter's hand, and they start their journey back home. As they pass the colorful flowers, Lisa stops.

"They are much prettier than my bouquet," Nele says sadly, but Lisa crouches beside her daughter. "They're not at all," she asserts. "This morning, you wanted to show me these flowers, right?" she asks, and Nele nods. "And I didn't have time to look at them. I only noticed them on the bus, and I was pretty sad we didn't see them together. But these flowers," she says, pointing to the grass in her hand. "These grass flowers belong to me alone. Everyone passing by the park can see the colorful, beautiful flowers. But my grass flowers are all mine. Because you wanted me to see something beautiful today, too." Nele's eyes light up. "So, the flowers in the park aren't prettier?" she asks, and Lisa shakes her head. "They're truly beautiful," she says. "But I got this grass of love from my daughter. These are much more beautiful. And the next time you want to show me something, I'll look. I promise!"

7. The Headache

As Emelie sees the phone number on her phone, she feels heat rush to her cheeks. Her pulse quickens, and she can't leave the open-plan office fast enough. "Yes?" she answers, and she can hear the slight trembling in her voice even in that one word. Because when her son's elementary school calls, it usually doesn't mean anything good. The school principal's first sentence confirms her fears. "Mrs. Meyer, please don't be alarmed. Nothing serious has happened." A chill runs down Emelie's spine because when someone says nothing serious has happened, it usually precedes the word 'but.'

"But it would be good if you could come to the school." Emelie closes her eyes momentarily, hearing the principal's next words from a distance. "Theo fell from the climbing frame during break time. He landed awkwardly on his leg. It's likely his leg is broken, which is why we've already called an ambulance." Before the principal can continue, Emelie rushes back to the office, grabs her jacket and bag, retrieves her keys, and whispers to her colleague that it's an emergency and she'll explain everything later. "Please get here safely," the principal urges over the phone. "Theo is being taken care of, and I don't want anything to happen to you on your way over here." But, of course, the principal's words are of no use to Emelie. She can just visualize her son sitting on the playground, crying, in pain, and feeling alone. She can see her child curled up, calling for her, feeling alone. Emelie pushes the accelerator. Nothing and no one can stop her from rushing to her injured child as quickly as possible.

In any other situation, her childlike imagination would have magically put an imaginary cape on her car and a rear sticker that read, "Supermom on Board." But not today. Today, dark thoughts prevail.

Just before she reaches the school, a brief, bright flashes as she drives along. But Emelie isn't surprised by this because Supermom has a mission, and that takes precedence over everything else.

"Theo?" Emelie is already calling her son's name from a distance. But unlike expected, her son isn't crying. His eyes are red, but the tears have long since dried up. Emelie scoops him up in her arms, strokes his head, and kisses him on the forehead. "Moooom." he nags, upset. "Not in front of my friends." Emelie laughs out. The fact that her son is embarrassed by her hug is more than fine with her now.

Minutes later, mom and son are sitting in the ambulance. "What am I going to do with you?" Emelie asks, looking at Theo disapprovingly. She turns to the paramedic. "You should know that I didn't give birth to a child but a dare-devil. I can't even count how many times this boy has come home injured. If I could, I would wrap him in cotton wool and only let him leave the house like that. Then, at least, nothing would happen to him." The paramedic winks at Theo. "Look here," he says, rolling up his jacket sleeve. A thick scar appears. "This break gave my mom quite a few nerves back in the day. I fell from a tree." Next, he takes off his shoe and points to his four toes. "Unfortunately, the fifth one was lost when I rode my bicycle barefoot and crashed into a wall so hard that it got torn off. That was the last straw for my mom." Now, he points to his forehead, where a crack in the skull is visible behind the skin on closer examination. "I did a forward somersault from the monkey bars. They were too high for me, and I split my skull on the ground. And because my mom had no nerves left to be robbed of, she lost her mind over it."

The paramedic looks at Emelie and winks at her, too. "There are minor and major accidents in a child's life. It's tough for parents. I can only advise you to keep your cool. Because worrying too much won't be in your child's best interest." Emelie smiles. She understands what the paramedic is trying to tell her. She won't be able to prevent everything. The most important thing is that Supermom is there when it matters. As Emelie looks out the window, she spots the speed camera on the side of the road. She remembers the flash she noticed on the way there. And she knows this ride in her Supermom-mobile will cost her more than just a few nerves this time.

8. The Superchild

"When I was one and a half years old, my mom was repeatedly asked a question," says Daniel Walter as he stands in front of the parents and students of his graduating class. He spent a long time polishing his speech, revising it over and over again and rewriting whole paragraphs. But finally, he has found the words he is determined to share as class president.

"How can it be that your boy can't walk yet? Do you think something's wrong with him?" Daniel hears some subdued laughter. "I see that some of you can relate to my mom," he adds, receiving agreement from several rows.

"When I got older, my mom would hear, at every meeting with other moms, how far their children had advanced beyond me. They could already say their names, eat independently, walk to school on their own at the age of four, fly to the moon, and change the world from up there. But I couldn't do any of that. I could only do what a child my age typically could. By then, I had learned to walk, say a few words, and put some food into my mouth with some effort, and poop in my diaper whenever I wanted." Daniel looks at his own mom, who he has spotted in the audience.

"Now, my mom had two choices. She had to decide whether to accept me as I was: a perfectly normal child, maybe a bit slower than other kids my age. Or she could have turned me into a superchild like her friends' kids. She could have pushed me in every way, put shoes in front of me to teach me how to put them on, sat me on a balance bike until I could balance properly, and place me in a spaceship so I could change the world from the moon. And my mom made up her mind."

Daniel lets his gaze sweep across the parents and his classmates. "She let me set the pace. She allowed me to grow and develop at my own tempo. And how often did she say to me that the other children were faster than me? How often did she notice the other children doing something I couldn't even think of? But that was all okay. I started school later than planned. I learned at my own pace and so missed one or two lessons. And yet, here I am today, holding a graduation certificate." Daniel proudly holds up his certificate and receives roaring applause. When the room quietens, he speaks the last words of his speech.

"I don't want to say at this point that children shouldn't be encouraged. I don't want to accuse my mom of that, either. She was always by my side, motivating and supporting me. But she left the tempo up to me. She didn't push me and never demanded more from me than I could've achieved. When I talk to other kids my age today, I sometimes hear that they'd like to have had an easier, carefree childhood:

less pressure to perform and more freedom. This freedom was given to me. And I still became something. I wish that every child could've had a mom like mine. A mom who let her child grow without pressuring him, through love and patience."

As Daniel looks at his mom again, he sees the tears in her eyes. "At some point, my mom began quoting an African proverb whenever she was told how slow I was compared to the other kids. And this proverb is what I want to pass on to every parent and my classmates for their journey ahead. Because I believe we all have the right to continue developing at our own pace."

Daniel sees his mom's lips move together with his as he recites the proverb that will always stay with him:

"Grass doesn't grow any faster if you pull on it."

9. A Perfect Christmas

"Honey, did you cook the potatoes?" Theresa hears the eye-rolling tone already in her husband's voice, "You've reminded me about a hundred times. Of course, I've cooked the potatoes." Theresa breathes a sigh of relief. The day before Christmas had been incredibly stressful, and if she had to put the potatoes on now, she would've fallen right into the saucepan out of pure exhaustion.

"Mommy, are Grandma and Grandpa coming early tomorrow?" she hears her son's voice through the baby monitor. Theresa groans. Felix should've fallen asleep by now. "Please tell me I'm so tired that I'm hallucinating Felix's voice." But when she sees her husband's apologetic eyes, she sighs. "That's all I need. Now he'll be awake for hours."

Theresa has been sitting with her son for what feels like an eternity when she hears his voice again, "And baked cookies." She looks at him with surprise, only to widen her eyes in shock. She listed the things she did today, not just in her thoughts but out loud. "It's time to sleep now," she says firmly. And when her son still doesn't close his eyes, she adds, "Or else Santa Claus won't come tomorrow." Immediately, as Felix clenches his eyes shut, she feels guilty. She had never threatened that Santa Claus wouldn't come. Santa has always been something wonderful in her home, something Felix could look forward to, no exception.

"That was nonsense," she admits. But still, her son doesn't open his tiny eyes. "With sauce," she adds, and now Felix peeks out from under his lashes. "Santa Claus will come tomorrow, just like in the years before." "Promise?" Felix asks, and Theresa nods. "Promise," she says, stroking his hair until she finally falls asleep in bed.

When she wakes up the next morning, she's lying next to her son, who tucked her in at some point during the night. And she also figures out the reason she has woken up, even though it's still dark outside. "It's Christmas, Mommy," Felix beams at her. Theresa couldn't tell how long he'd been staring at her; she was sure it was him who woke her up with his piercing gaze.

Theresa jumps out of bed, runs to the door, back to her son, lifts him up in her arms, spins him around, wishes him a Merry Christmas, and then rushes back out the door and down the stairs. There's certainly a lot to do before her parents arrive.

She shakes her head again once she glances at the Christmas tree. She had envisioned an elegant tree with golden ornaments and a tree topper resembling an angel. However, Felix had broken the topper on the floor the day before. He'd cried terribly—almost as much as his mom, who, sniffling, had rummaged through the Christmas box to find the wooden ornaments to hang on the tree.

The fact that the fancy bread she intended to serve with the sausages had burnt during that time didn't make the situation any better. Standing in the living room, she could still smell the strong smell of burnt bread. She'd convinced herself that potato salad was almost as good as bread. But, if she was honest with herself, it felt like a lousy second choice.

Theresa examines the room to observe the evidence of all the mishaps from the past few days. Parts of the Christmas decorations were torn because Felix ran through them. The floor was sparkling because Theresa's husband had sneezed while trying to make the Christmas train sparkle. The gingerbread house was long gone, even though Theresa had forbidden anyone to nibble on it before Christmas. All she wants is to make up for all that today; after all, it's supposed to be a perfect Christmas.

"It's perfect," she suddenly hears her son's soft voice behind her. Startled, Theresa turns around. "Really?" she asks, seeing her son's eyes sparkle. "Yesterday was just a bit rubbish, and I want today to be much nicer," says Felix, looking at his mom hopefully. A smile finally spreads across her face, too. Her son is absolutely right that yesterday was pretty lousy. It wasn't about every detail being perfect or every plan going smoothly. Instead, it was about being together and spending time with each other.

"CRASH!" Theresa and Felix flinch as they hear a loud bang from the kitchen. It gets worse when her husband calls from the kitchen. "Theresa? Can you come here for a moment? Still, she remains relaxed because she knows nothing can spoil her mood today.

10. With Love and Protection

"How old are you, little one?" Miriam feels her daughter hiding behind her legs. "Come on, tell us how old you are," the woman they met in the park presses her again. "Stella's a bit shy. She's already four," Miriam apologizes, sensing her daughter clinging to her legs. But in the very next second, she regrets it. Her daughter isn't shy at all; she's quite an outgoing child. But something about the woman standing in front of them seems to make her feel uneasy. Miriam says goodbye to the woman and takes her daughter's hand again.

"Oh my, what a sweet little thing you are." On this particular day, it's an elderly lady who, at the very same moment, gently strokes Stella's cheek. "And those golden curls are absolutely beautiful." Almost in an instant, the elderly lady pulls away her hand and disappears. Miriam looks at her daughter, seeing the unease in Stella's eyes, and again, she's annoyed with herself for not intervening in time.

"Stella, remember, we made a deal that you could choose only one treat today. That's it for today." As Miriam looks at her daughter while shopping, she can't help but see the sadness in her eyes. She feels herself softening under her daughter's gaze. "Alright," she says. "You can have one more treat. But that's it for today." Miriam hears the voice of a young woman behind her. "How inconsistent," the woman whispers to her partner, and Miriam feels herself blushing. "Although," she says, looking sternly at her daughter, "we made an agreement, didn't we? We said there would be one treat, and that's what we're sticking with today." Seeing the tears forming in Stella's eyes, she feels a little more ashamed.

Stella, we need to go home." Miriam calls her daughter, who is sitting on the swing, laughing out loud. "In a minute, Mommy," Stella calls, and Miriam waits a moment before calling out another time. "Just a bit longer!" Stella begs, but this time, Miriam shakes her head. "We have to leave now; we're already running late," she says. As Stella jumps off the swing, she stomps her foot in a huff. "I don't want to," she says, with anger rising. Before Miriam can respond, her daughter starts jumping up and down, screaming, and entering tantrum mode. "You look really ugly when you scream like that," Miriam hears a woman's voice behind her. Stella stops her brief tantrum, fizzling out just as it had started. She reaches for her mom's hand as the woman starts to leave – but this time, Miriam refuses to have regrets. Although her heart pounds inside her chest, she has no intention of staying calm.

"And you think you can tell my child that she is ugly?" She asks loudly, making sure everyone at the playground can hear her. "I just wanted to," the woman protests, but Miriam doesn't let her finish. "Let me tell you what's ugly. It's ugly to reprimand other people's kids. It's ugly to grab their face without asking first. It's ugly to expect answers from them when they're not supposed to talk to strangers. No child is ugly; it's the adults who are. And what you just said was especially ugly."

Miriam turns around and holds her daughter's hand a little tighter. "We're going home, Stella," she says. "And I'm right here with you!" she adds. Because she has learned one thing: she is responsible for protecting her child. She is the one who must shield her from the intrusiveness of some adults. She'll never again feel ashamed for not being brave enough to protect her daughter.

11. A Child's Mouth

"A man?" Frederike points to the man standing by the shelf in the store, and her mom, Diana, nods. "Exactly," she says. "That's a man." Frederike looks around curiously. "A woman?" she asks, already nodding in agreement. Once again, Diana confirms what her daughter has guessed. Throughout their shopping trip, the three-year-old girl categorizes the people she sees into "a man" and "a woman." And Diana repeatedly gives her confirmation, even at the checkout. In the corner of her eye, Diana notices an elderly woman standing behind her, wearing a hat and a long, flowing skirt. Her daughter continues slowly assigning genders to each person she sees at the checkout as Diana nods and confirms her guesses. But just before Frederike reaches the woman behind Diana, the mom feels a change in her child. She notices her eyes widen, alarmed, and then suddenly feels her arm grabbing her. In a loud voice, Frederike exclaims, "An evil witch!"

Diana flinches and closes her eyes. It feels like it's never been quieter at the checkout. She feels all eyes on her and can't wait to get out of there.

When Diana tells her friend Denise about the incident, Denise can't stop laughing. "And what did the evil witch say?" she asks, but Diana shrugs with a laugh. "I didn't look at her," she admits. Denise touches her friend's arm and shares what her son John did recently.

"You know my fear of bees, right?" she says. And, of course, Diana can vividly picture Denise dancing wildly on the street when she comes in contact with bees in the summer. "John has developed a fear of them too; I've done a great job of training him to be," Denise says, rolling her eyes, aware that children often inherit their parents' fears when exposed to them frequently. "Anyway, Martin has finally put-up fly screens. Lately, I could always calm John down when we'd have bees by the window. "The bees are outside; I'd say when he was about to run away."

Denise shakes her head, recalling what John shouted at her in the street. "So, the other day, while we were walking through town, a bee came flying at me; I was already drawing enough attention by wildly flailing my arms around. John tried to remind me that the bees were outside." Diana already senses what's coming. She knows what John is like with his little speech impediment. "Anyway, he was about to say 'Mama, bee here, bee here, bee here!', but instead he screamed at the top of his lungs, in front of all the people already watching me: "Mom, queer, queer, queer!" It was like a demonstration against homosexual couples." Diana feels the coffee she just drank shoot up her nose. Tears come to her eyes as the burning liquid spreads in her nasal passages.

Denise shrugs. "I think our kids will embarrass us plenty of times in the future. In any case, I bowed to my audience, explaining that I'm not homophobic and am open to all relationships, and then we continued walking. I think they all thought I was crazy, but that's fine. You know the saying - 'Once your reputation is ruined...'" Diana has finally managed to get the last drops of coffee out of her nose into a tissue. "At some point, we'll embarrass our kids just as much as they do us," she laughs, rubbing her hands together. "I, for one, will kiss Frederike in front of all her school friends." Denise adds, "With snot that you'll smear on her cheek in front of everyone." Diana continues her playful planning.

"And then I'll point to a boy and ask her if he's the one she's in love with." Diana holds out her pinky to Denise, who Denise playfully hooks her finger back.

"The revenge of all those embarrassments will be sweet," they say, knowing that they'll never embarrass their children as much as it happens all too often the other way around.

12. The Colorful Dog

"I don't want to dress up," Henriette says, crossing her arms over her chest and looking sternly at her mom, Svenja. "And I told you that from the very beginning."

Svenja stands there with the self-sewn costume in her hand and shakes her head. She had to admit that Henriette did say she didn't need a costume when the school party was announced. However, she'd expected it to be a passing whim that had led Henriette to say that. She thought her daughter would be sad to be the only child without a costume at the school party. So, she'd sat at the sewing machine and crafted an elaborate costume.

"But you love Elsa," Svenja tries one more time. However, Henriette's arms remain crossed over her chest. "Yes," she admits. "But I don't want to be dressed up like Elsa. I want to go to school as Henriette."

Svenja puts all her powers of persuasion into the next sentence. "But you realize you'll be the only child not dressed up, right? You'll stand out from everyone else, like a colorful dog among a bunch of brown dogs." Henriette shrugs. "That's okay," she says, putting her backpack on. "Henriette," Svenja pleads and makes one last attempt. "I put so much effort into this. I'd be sad if you didn't wear the costume today." She sees her daughter's shoulders stiffen. The girl takes a deep breath and nods. "Okay, Mom," she says, chucking her bag on the ground. Svenja claps her hands excitedly. She knows her daughter will look absolutely beautiful in the costume, and Henriette will surely realize that, too.

It's not long before Svenja is standing in front of the mirror with her daughter. "And? What do you think?" she asks hopefully. "Great," says Henriette and offers her mom a faint smile. At this moment, Svenja notices that her daughter's laughter isn't as carefree as usual. 'She just needs a little time to get used to the costume. She'll be excited to wear it soon,' she tells herself.

"Come on, we need to get going," she urges her Elsa-dressed daughter. She quickly takes a photo, and then they're on their way. But on the way to school, Henriette is unusually quiet. "Don't you like the costume?" Svenja asks, glancing in the rear-view mirror. "Yes," her daughter says, shrugging. "But I also don't mind being a colorful dog." Svenja watches as Henriette fiddles with the sleeves of her dress – her little blonde daughter who, at this moment, looks nothing like herself.

"Please excuse our lateness." Svenja apologizes to the teacher as she and Henriette finally arrive at school. "But this morning, both of us had to deal with quite some stubbornness." The teacher looks at Henriette and nods in understanding, as she is quite familiar with how stubborn her students can be on some days. "And did you manage to figure it out?" she asks. Svenja nods. "After a lot of fuss, I finally realized that I'd simply ignored my daughter's wish not to dress up. She managed to rid me of my stubbornness." The teacher looks at Svenja in astonishment, and Svenja winks at her daughter. "Have lots of fun, my little colorful dog," she says, leaving the classroom. She leaves her daughter as the only one not dressed up and, therefore, the most noticeable girl in the class. And she is incredibly proud. Because her child dares to stand out from the crowd when she doesn't feel like doing something, she has made a decision about her own body and defended it to her mom. Never again will Svenja try to manipulate her child by claiming that Henriette would make her sad with her choice. She understands that her daughter is already where Svenja would like her to be capable of expressing her own opinions, defending them, and setting boundaries by making decisions for herself. These are qualities that will undoubtedly serve her well in her future life.

13. Parents' Evening

"Good evening. I take it you're Mrs. Sauer?" the kindergarten teacher asks Emelie with a smile. "That's correct. I'm so happy to be here," the young mom responds with a smile. She had hurried from work to make it to her son's kindergarten parent-teacher evening. She'd rushed and even had to ask her boss if she could leave an hour earlier. "We finally have a face to put to Steve's Mom," the kindergarten teacher adds, and Emelie takes a seat without responding, feeling somewhat out of place. She doesn't typically get intimidated so easily, but when dealing with her son's teachers, she has no idea how to behave. She doesn't want potential conflicts to affect her son.

"Wouldn't it make much more sense to fasten the sides with a bracket? That way, we wouldn't have to wait for the glue to dry. It would also make it more stable," Emelie suggests to another mom as they work on a birdhouse together after the kindergarten teachers' presentation. It's supposed to be a surprise for the children, who are currently involved in a spring project. "Oh," she hears the voice of the teacher from earlier behind her. "I'd completely forgotten that we have a specialist among us. Steve mentioned you work in a trade profession.

Nevertheless, I think a birdhouse for a kindergarten doesn't necessarily have to be made by a tradie." The kindergarten teacher begins to walk away, clearing her throat, and says, "Please forgive me. I meant by a professional, of course." Emelie raises an eyebrow but swallows her anger once again.

She and her husband had consciously chosen their current lifestyle when Steve was born. Emelie had wished to get back to her beloved job as soon as possible, and her husband had wanted to stay home and be with Steve. They'd always encountered surprised faces due to this arrangement but had never experienced this level of disapproval that Emelie senses today.

As Emelie says her goodbyes at the end of the parent-teacher evening, a slightly crooked but completed birdhouse stands in the middle of the room. "See?" the kindergarten teacher asks with a smile. "I told you that a simple birdhouse is enough for our children. I don't think the birds will reject the food because the birdhouse is slightly lopsided. Your husband can tell you tomorrow how happy the children will be. After all, he always brings the boy to the group and gets to witness the joy you miss." Emelie shakes her head. There's no way she can stay silent now. "You really believe I'm not interested in my son?" The teacher grins a little wider and raises her hands in defense. "I never claimed that Mrs. Sauer," she says, but Emelie refuses to let her get away with it. "Your insinuations tonight were enough," she says. "You disapprove of our lifestyle, and we can see that. Even my husband knows what you think of us." The kindergarten teacher raises her eyebrows, but Emelie holds her own. "Even though you probably don't think it, we function like any other family. When I come home from work, both Steve and my husband tell me about their day. We exchange stories and spend all evening together. We play games, have dinner, and talk. I'd even go so far as to claim that my son loves me just as much as other children love their moms. Just because something doesn't conform to the conventional worldview doesn't mean it's bad or wrong."

When Emelie turns around and feels a hand on her shoulder, she recognizes a mom who had been sitting next to her while making the birdhouse. "Sometimes, I wish I were as brave as you," she admits. Emelie stops in surprise. "Brave?" she asks, and the mom nods. "We also considered whether we could imagine my husband staying at home while I work. We both could've seen it working well. But we didn't dare. We were afraid that we would face some resistance. I think a lot of the moms who were here tonight look up to you and your husband because you have the courage to swim against the tide."

As Emelie gets into her car, she can't get the mom's words out of her mind. She'd never seen herself as a role model. It gave her hope because she knows that, alongside the people who rigidly cling to old structures, there are also those who are open-minded and open to alternatives. When she kisses her sleeping boy on the forehead that night, he reaches for her arm, and she says, "Mommy is home, my sweetie. And I'm always here for you."

14. A Number of Tissues

"Finally, we've made it," Frida says directly after her mom picks up the phone. Tired and exhausted, she collapses onto the sofa. "So, how'd it go?" Trudi asks, having been waiting for her daughter's call for a while. "It went okay," Frida admits. "Today, Mathilda stayed at kindergarten alone for the first time. There were quite a few tears, but now I'm finally home."

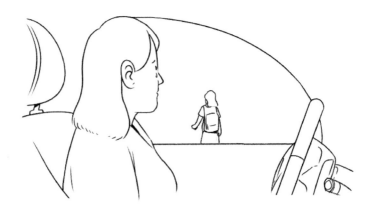

Frida hears the emerging pause clearly. "Tears?" Trudi finally asks, and Frida closes her eyes. "Yes," she confirms.

"They just wouldn't stop running. But now they're gone, and I think everything will be fine." Frida waits, and the question she expected follows promptly. "I hope Mathilda didn't notice that you cried. That might confuse her."

Frida laughs out loud. She knew, of course, that her mom would immediately understand what had happened. After all, Mathilda had always been a very independent and tough girl. "Come on, Mom, really," Frida chides. "I still have some dignity left in me." Then she mumbles, "I waited to cry until the car door was closed." Frida hears her mom's high-pitched, bell-like voice laughing through the phone. "You've always been emotional," she says. "The tears you've shed in your life would probably last your daughter's life. That's probably why she cries so rarely."

Frida crosses her arms over her chest, even if her mom can't see it. Pouting, she says, "I know I'm a softy. But seriously, Mathilda just wandered off without even turning around to say 'bye' to me. I was standing at the door and was the only one waving while all the other moms were trying to encourage their tearful children. I want a teary-eyed child too, one that won't let go of me. I just want a child who misses me." Once again, Frida hears the silence on the other end. "You're right," she admits. "I don't want Mathilda to cry at all. I just want her to miss me." Again, Trudi doesn't respond. Frida rolls her eyes. "You have to stop with the aggressive silence. I also know that all I basically want for my daughter is to have fun and get along great without me. Is that all right now?" Finally, Trudi responds, "There you go," she says. "There's a spark of emotional intelligence in you, after all." Frida takes a deep breath, about to go on the offensive, but her mom beats her to it. "Well," she explains, "you've always been very driven by your emotions. How many things did you miss as a child because you couldn't detach yourself from me? You used to cry so much that I had to take you out of school trips, sign you out of holiday camps, and pick you up from class outings. And even though it's hard for you to let go of Mathilda, you'll quickly realize how wonderful it is that she doesn't have these difficulties. She'll be much freer than you were as a child." Frida clicks her tongue sarcastically. "Well then," she says curtly. "I'm going to have to get off the phone and do some housework. After all, it won't do itself." Frida hears the smile in her mom's voice as she says goodbye. As she hangs up, she smiles. Of course, she knows her mom is absolutely right. And her mom knows that she fully knows it. In mutual agreement, they decided long ago that she'd probably always remain the softy.

"Mommy!" Mathilda calls out as Frida arrives at the kindergarten. Her little girl jumps into her arms. "I did some crafting and played, and I was outside, and I made a sand cake, and Timo ate it – really, he ate my sand cake for real." Frida beams at her daughter. "Then you really had a lot of fun. I'm so happy for you!" And just as she says it, Frida means it. She knows there's nothing better than her daughter enjoying her time, even if it means she forgets her Mommy for a few hours.

15. By All Means Necessary

"And that means that the static friction between the road surface and the tire is responsible for the car rolling. Without this friction, the tire would slide and have no reason to rotate," Brenda looks into her daughter's eyes. "Do you finally understand it now? It's quite simple, and I don't understand why I must explain it to you again today. It seems to me like you just don't want to understand it." Brenda hears her husband's voice from the hallway. "Just give up on it," he says with a laugh. "She won't understand what static friction is and how it works in the coming weeks either. Somehow, the part responsible for logic in your Mom's brain was forgotten." Brenda is about to rant when her daughter adds another layer. "But Dad," she sighs, "this really isn't that hard. I've tried a thousand times to explain it to Mom, but she just refuses to get it."

Brenda stands up and tosses her long hair behind her. "Oh really," she says and leaves the kids' room. "What would I do if you two weren't always so in agreement?" Grinning, she walks downstairs. As she always does when she's feeling a little frustrated, she grabs her large mixing bowl, flour, sugar, and the other ingredients she needs. Baking allows Brenda to relax, detach from her thoughts, and let her other senses take over. Of course, she knows she's smart enough to understand her daughter's schoolwork and help her when she needs it – at least when it's not physics, a subject she's always detested. Fortunately, her husband is skilled enough in that area to support their daughter if she has any questions. However, Brenda doesn't really expect that to happen because their daughter seems to be a physics prodigy. She effortlessly explains physical concepts, can develop her thoughts, disproves or proves theories, and formulates clever reasoning independently. Brenda's husband sometimes affectionately calls the girl "Little Miss Einstein," which makes Brenda especially proud, even though she herself struggles with whether or not to put up the handbrake when parking on a slight incline.

"Wow, that smells delicious," Brenda hears her daughter's voice before she even hears the patter of hurried footsteps on the stairs. She has finished baking the cookies, and without any trace of arrogance, she admits they've turned out better than ever before. The little cookies are beautifully round, and the subtle hint of cinnamon doesn't overshadow the vanilla that Brenda has skillfully added.

"Enjoy," Brenda says as she slides the cookie plate over to her husband. They all happily dig in. "I want some ice cream with it," Brenda suddenly exclaims. "Walnut ice cream would go perfectly with the cinnamon and vanilla." She jumps up and scoops a few ice cream balls onto the plates before sitting back down. As her husband and daughter continue to discuss her non-existent knowledge of physics, she contemplates throwing a cookie at them. The round treat bounces on the table and rolls over to her daughter. "That didn't work," Brenda says, attempting it again a second time. But this time, she accidentally nudges the ice cream dish with her arm. The now-melted ice cream spills across the table, and the cookie, which was simultaneously speeding over the tabletop, slides across the liquid like it's on an ice rink. Brenda's eyes widen. She looks at her daughter and her husband, realizing that all three of them are thinking the same thing. "There's no such thing!" Brenda laughs and slaps her forehead. "Aquaplaning!"

Brenda's daughter looks questioningly at her mom, but Brenda shakes her head while laughing.

"You went to so much trouble to explain to me the concept of friction. You and your father both made fun of me. And yet, I finally understand what you mean when you say the lack of friction is responsible for sliding. But I think you're smart enough to figure out what all of this has to do with 'aquaplaning.' And until you do, I'm going to relish the fact that I know more about physics than you." As Brenda stuffs a cookie into her mouth, a smile spreads across her lips – only to disappear at her daughter's words. "Isn't aquaplaning the sliding of tires on a road when there's a layer of water on it?"

16. The Perspective of Two Moms

"Look, I bought Dorina a little baby nest," Irmi says, smiling at her daughter. However, Miriam rolls her eyes. "Mom," she explains, sounding a tad condescending. "People haven't used nests for years. It hinders air circulation and is suspected of causing sudden infant death syndrome." Irmi lowers her arms, holding the small piece of fabric with beautiful white lace between her fingers. "Really?" she asks, looking surprised. "I didn't know that." Miriam looks at her precociously once again. "Times have changed since I was born. I've told you that so many times. In my book 'Good Parents, Good Children,' I've read everything about what people do nowadays. I'll manage, you can be sure of that. Now, I need to go to the kitchen and cook."

Irmi nods. That's clearly her cue to leave. Because this new trend of taking the placenta home after giving birth and eating it is something she finds more than a little repulsive. "Is that another tip from 'Good Parents, Good Children'?" she asks her daughter, who nods enthusiastically. "The book is worth its weight in gold, Mom. I won't find better advice anywhere else," she says happily and heads to the kitchen.

As Irmi leaves her daughter's and grandchild's house, she feels worried and a little sad. Her daughter, who was only 18 years old, came to her in tears when she found out she was pregnant. Irmi assured her she'd be by her side and support her whenever she needed. At first, the two of them talked a lot, made plans, and looked forward to little Dorina's arrival. But then, Miriam received this dreaded book, and from that point on, a lot changed. Miriam believed she was perfectly prepared for pregnancy, childbirth, and the time afterward. Miriam and her unborn child became water beings together, communicating on a mental level through baby talk, and even had the umbilical cord frozen in case the stem cells were needed one day.

"Modern stuff," mutters Irmi to herself. Of course, she doesn't want to question the changes brought about in the last 18 years regarding pregnancy and childbirth. Of course, she didn't know that it was best to let babies sleep on their backs for better air circulation. Nor was she aware that the use of the little nest was discouraged. But did a few lines on 100 pages really offer more knowledge, experience, and tips than what she could offer her daughter? Irmi doubts it. She believes her daughter has grown into a pretty respectful young adult. Even when she found out she was unexpectedly pregnant, she made the best of the situation, accepted the challenge, and managed it.

Lost in thought, Irmi runs her fingers over the lace of the little nest. She'll make a bonnet or a small summer dress out of it; she's sure of that. So deep in thought she almost doesn't hear her phone ringing. "Mom?" she hears Miriam's tense voice right after answering the call. "Can you please come?"

Irmi doesn't ask questions. She doesn't dwell on the harsh way her daughter dismissed her only an hour ago. She gets up and heads over. When she arrives, she sees the tears in Miriam's eyes. "What happened?" she asks, already expecting the worst. "She just won't stop crying, no matter what I do. I did a baby massage, stroked her belly, and applied sensory and breathing techniques. I connected with her mentally, but it seems like I'm not getting through. I don't know what to do."

Irmi walks past her daughter to her tiny grandchild. "May I?" she asks, waiting for her daughter's nod. She lifts the little baby into her arms and gently rocks her. She hums a little tune, and instantly, the cries subside. "It's unbelievable," says Miriam as she realizes the obvious solution. She takes her baby from her mom and continues to sway; she remains quiet and relaxed. Irmi looks to her daughter, who smiles gratefully. "I wouldn't know what I'd do without you," Miriam whispers to her. And there it is the feeling that she and her daughter can continue on this journey together, as new knowledge and old wisdom complement each other.

17. Sea of Broken Glass

"I can't believe this, Anna. I've told you a hundred times that you're not supposed to be here." Emilia gazes at the clay vase that's shattered on the living room floor. It's the vase her mom gave her just before her death. And it's the vase that Anna has always found so beautiful, as if it held some pull of magical attraction. With her arms crossed behind her back, Anna stands still and doesn't move an inch as Emilia continues to scold her, "You're five years old, and I thought I could rely on you to do as I say." Carefully, Anna picks up each shard, one by one, and places them in a bowl. "I'll never be able to piece it back together," she says, dejected and setting the bowl of shards on the countertop. Emilia gets the hoover and thoroughly cleans the living room. She hears the little shards clinking as the vacuum sucks them up. When she's finished, she sees her daughter standing at the same spot with her arms behind her back. "Don't you want to play anymore?" she asks, but Anna shakes her head and looks down. Emilia kneels beside her daughter, taking her in her arms. "I shouldn't have scolded you so much," she admits, feeling her daughter's tear drop onto her hand. She continues in, "But you see, I did tell you so many times not to touch the vase because it's important to me. And you did it anyway. Now it's broken, and I don't think I'll be able to fix it. What did you want to do with the vase anyway?"

Anna finally brings her arms out from behind her back. She holds a small bouquet of daisies she must have collected while playing in the garden. Emilia feels a lump in her throat forming. "Did you pick those for me?" she asks, and her daughter nods. "I wanted to make you happy," Anna explains, shrugging her small shoulders. "But I made you sad. I'm sorry." Emilia closes her eyes for a moment. She now regrets scolding her daughter.

"I need to apologize to you, too," she admits. "I told you off too harshly and made you sad. I think it's really sweet you wanted to make me happy." Emilia stands up, takes her daughter's hand, and fetches a glass from the cupboard, filling it with water. "Would you like to put the flowers in there?" she asks, offering her daughter the small substitute vase. Then, the two of them place the flowers on the dining table. This gives Emilia an idea. As an avid crafter, she already has everything she needs at home.

"What do you think about making a beautiful mosaic together with the shards?" she asks, noticing her daughter's eyes light up. "But you have to be very careful because the shards are sharp, okay? Clay is not as sharp as glass, but we both need to be cautious." Emilia and Anna carefully glue one clay shard after another onto a wooden board. Gradually, they create a beautiful and colorful mosaic. After all the pieces are placed, Emilia seals the mosaic with glue. "Now we have to let it dry, and afterward, we can apply some varnish to make it shine. How do you like our mosaic?" Anna's eyes sparkle as she gently runs her fingers over the individual pieces. "It's prettier than the vase," she says, smiling at her mom. As Emilia gazes at the mosaic, she realizes her daughter is right. The vase's structure can be seen much clearer in the image. But that's not the only thing that becomes clear to her: there are days when things don't go smoothly when something even breaks. However, with some time, effort, and patience, something messy can be transformed into something wonderful - and not just when it comes to vases.

18. With All The Frills

Supermom takes one last look in the mirror. Her cape billows behind her in waves, the mask fits snugly, and her hair is perfectly in place. The knee-high boots cling firmly to her feet, and her gloves are pulled up to her elbows. "Here we go again," Supermom says to her reflection and takes off. She zooms through the house, gives her daughter a quick kiss in flight, and gets her first grumble of the day. "I want to sleep longer," the seven-year-old girl whines, but Supermom shakes her head. "Wake up, princess," she lovingly instructs the child and receives the next bout of complaining. "You're mean," the girl grumbles, standing up and stomping off to the bathroom. And Supermom? She swallows her first surge of emerging emotions.

"You still need to wash my lunchbox," the child grumbles at the breakfast table, pulling the container from her school backpack. However, Supermom had already beaten her to it. "I put a fresh one out for you, and I'll wash this one later," she says, but the girl shakes her head. "But this one is my favorite, and I want to take it with me," the girl insists. Supermom takes a deep breath and washes the lunchbox. She wants so much to make her child happy – what's a little washing up in the morning? But as she hands over the filled clean lunchbox, the girl casually tosses it into her school backpack without much attention. Supermom tilts her head, but when the girl looks at her questioningly, she turns away. She doesn't want the child to realize that she's currently upset and a little sad. A Supermom doesn't show her true emotions; she is always cheerful and there for her children.

When the girl returns from school in the afternoon, her trousers are ripped. "It happened accidentally while I was sliding," she says, changing her trousers in a flash and leaving her torn trousers on the floor. Supermom is a little exhausted. She has spent the entire morning cleaning the house, shopping, and fitting a new tire onto her daughter's bike. Supermom is feeling worn out, but when her daughter looks at her, she puts on a smile. "No problem," she says and picks up the trousers from the floor. "I'll put a cool patch on there. You'll like it." Supermom jumps up from the floor and swiftly flies to her craft box. She searches for a patch, flies back, quickly sews it onto the trousers, and proudly shows them to the girl – who seems less than enthusiastic. "Mom," the girl says, shaking her head. "The patch isn't nice. Besides, those trousers were already too tight for me."

Supermom takes a deep breath. Her daughter could've mentioned this before she started working on it. However, when the girl looks at Supermom, she just shrugs. "I'll make something else out of the trousers, then," she says and is about to leave the room when she hears her daughter's voice. "But nothing embarrassing," she says.

At that moment, Supermom feels it happening. The cape rips off her back, the boots and gloves vanish, and the mask falls. In that moment, Supermom transforms into Lisa – just a regular mom.

"Christine?" she asks her daughter, who immediately notices the change in tone. "Don't you think you could be a bit more grateful?" Christin looks at her mom and furrows her eyebrows, but Lisa continues. "This morning, you told me off several times. When I washed your lunchbox, you didn't even say thank you. I'm pretty tired and worn out because I've been working the whole morning. I had to rush to get as much done as possible before you got home. Then I fixed your trousers, specifically, only to hear that they're too small for you anyway. And now you're accusing me of being embarrassing. Seriously: I'm tired, and right now, I feel pretty disappointed and annoyed. Can't you try and be a little friendlier for once?"

As Lisa leaves the room, she gathers her Supermom costume, which has been abandoned on the floor. Lisa isn't sure if she has what it takes to be a Supermom. She always wanted to be there for her daughter, be strong, and untouchable. But now, she has lost her mask and revealed her true self. Lisa  places the Supermom costume on the dining room chair. She's pretty sure she doesn't need it anymore.

A little while later, there's a knock-on Lisa's bedroom door. Christin enters and looks apologetically at her mom. "I wasn't nice," she admits. "You put in so much effort."

Christin gives her mom a kiss on the cheek and hands her the Supermom costume. "You are my Supermom," she says, and then disappears from the room. As Lisa slips into her outfit, she realizes that a Supermom doesn't always have to be in a good mood and untouchable. It's more about expressing emotions and admitting to feeling vulnerable. Supermom puts on her shoes, gloves, and cape, but puts away the mask, because she doesn't need it anymore.

19. That Makes Sense

"But you were on such a good path," Brigitte says, looking at Hanni with her long, fluttering eyelashes. "You were just promoted. I mean, you're 30 years old and could've become a junior executive. You'll probably never get another opportunity like this. Was this necessary right now?" Hanni takes a sip of her coffee and looks at her long-time friend. Lost in thought, she strokes her belly, which is starting to show a small bump. "It wasn't planned," she admits. "And I would've loved to have taken the promotion. We're already stretching our budget pretty thin. With the additional costs of a child but the same salary, it'll be quite tight. But we'll manage somehow." However, Brigitte is not satisfied with Hanni's explanation. "I'm not talking about whether you'll be able to afford it or not," she says. "I'm talking about all the opportunity you're going to miss. You've always been a career woman and set your sights high. Your chance has finally come around. Are you sure this is what you want?" Hanni looks into her friend's eyes and shrugs because she isn't sure that this is what she wants. But what choice does she have? Brigitte places her hand on her friend's arm as if she heard her thoughts: "You still have a choice. It's not too late."

Hanni suddenly stands up from the table. She's in her eleventh week of pregnancy, and although she was initially shocked at the idea of having a child, she'd never considered this option a choice. She briefly says goodbye to the woman who knows less about her than Hanni assumed. But over the following week, one thought that keeps creeping into her mind is, "You still have a choice. It's not too late."

A few weeks later, as usual, Hanni sets off to work early in the morning. Perfectly dressed and styled, she walks up the stairs to her office in high heels. When the phone on her desk rings, she answers with the company's slogan, handles the first inquiries of the workday, and then sits down at her desk. She loves her office and is perfectly suited for the customer relations she deals with daily. Hanni takes a look at her busy schedule. The coming weeks are packed with various appointments and meetings .

"Morning, can I come in?" The client scheduled for half-past eight that morning asks hesitantly at the door. She is heavily pregnant and cradles her belly with one hand. Hanni looks longingly at the round belly in which a baby has been growing for many weeks. "Of course," she says, gets up, adjusts a chair for the client, and sits back down. The conversation doesn't take long. The client quickly agrees with Hanni's advice, suggestions, and plans, so everything is wrapped up quickly.

"When is it due?" Hanni asks, gesturing to the client's belly. "In two weeks," she replies, struggling to put on her jacket. Hanni smiles at the baby bump. Seeing the client, she thinks about the decision she made a few weeks ago, and for her, it'd been the right one.

Hanni says goodbye to her client, closing the office door behind her. She sits at her desk and notes everything they'd discussed. As her fingers fly across the keyboard, she hears the familiar clicking sounds she is so used to. She is a career woman; there's no doubting that. Then, out of nowhere, it happens. Hanni lets out a little groan and places her hand on her belly. She feels the movement beneath her hand and freezes. That was it. The first kick from the little being growing inside her.

Yes, Hanni is a career woman, but in this moment, she recognizes the true meaning of her life more than ever. She knows her job will be waiting for her, but it's not her top priority. At this moment, it's all about the little baby growing inside her, and she looks forward to it more than anything else in the world.

20. Different Worlds

"Oh my God, do you need a tissue, wet wipes, or a cloth? I always have a cloth and a bit of water with me just in case something like this happens. I also have something to drink," the unfamiliar mom says, looking at Tamara with big, innocent eyes. "Thank you," says Tamara, shaking her head. "Dirt cleanses the stomach. Daniel can handle it." Then she turns back to her son, who she can see struggling to escape the sandpit. While sliding, he'd been catapulted into the sand and landed in the sand with a big thud, accidentally eating the sand in the process. The crunching sound of the sand between his growing teeth could be heard by Tamara all the way to the edge of the playground.

"I also have hand sanitizer," the unfamiliar mom offers helpfully again. Tamara smiles at the woman. "Should I rinse his mouth with it?" she asks ironically, winking at her. "In all seriousness, we'll manage, but thank you anyway." When Daniel has finally managed to get out of the sand, he runs over. "Eww, Mommy," he complains, and Tamara smiles at him. "Would you like a sip to drink?" she asks, handing her four-year-old son a bottle of apple juice. In the corner of her eye, she sees the shocked look on the young mom's face. By example, Tamara pops a piece of chocolate into her son's mouth. "Eat it carefully," she adds before smiling at the mom.

Tamara had already made up her mind and labeled the mom as overly protective, the classic helicopter mom. Before the mom has the chance to look away, Tamara licks the melted chocolate off her fingers and wipes the remainder on her trousers. For a brief moment, she fears the woman might faint, but fortunately, she's spared the ordeal.

"Bye," Tamara says half an hour later and is about to leave the playground with her son when another woman enters, pushing a wheelchair with a child sitting in it. The child's head is tilted at an unnaturally twisted angle, their eyes rolling back and forth. But, when the child sees the helicopter Mom, they excitedly clap their hands. Tamara turns to look at the three of them.

"My darling," the helicopter mom says, embracing her child. The child leans forward with happiness, trying to embrace their mom awkwardly. Tamara can't take her eyes off them. "We just passed a dog, and she stretched out her arm. I'm not entirely sure if she stroked it." The helicopter mom widens her eyes. "And did you disinfect her hands?" she asks, but the woman shakes her head apologetically. "That's why I'm telling you. The hand sanitizer spilled."

The helicopter mom takes a small tube from her bag, disinfects her daughter's hands, and thoroughly moisturizes her dry skin. "Next time I look after her, I'll bring a spare bottle just in case," the woman suggests, and the helicopter mom nods. Then, her gaze falls on Tamara by chance. "Immune deficiency," she explains, and Tamara nods.

As she takes her son's hand and leaves the playground, she feels guilty. Without knowing her, she'd labeled the stranger as a helicopter mom. However, knowing that her child has a disability and immune deficiency changes everything. "Excuse me?" she hears the woman's voice behind her. Tamara turns around and faces the woman once again. "Not such an overprotective mom as you initially thought, right?" she asks with a wink, and Tamara can feel herself blushing. "Don't worry. Most people immediately see me as an overprotective mom. And if I'm honest, I was that way even before Tammie was born. My older son still holds it over me. Still, I think that everyone should raise their child as they see fit, as long as it doesn't harm the child. If you'd like, we can meet tomorrow at the playground again tomorrow. I'll bring sugar-free cookies and unsweetened tea so your son can have something healthy to eat." Tamara laughs as the woman winks at her. Because good parenting can take so many different forms, and anything goes, as long as children and parents feel good about it.

21. Fartpoop

"In all seriousness," Jack's teacher says, lowering her voice as she whispers to his mom, "I wish there was a single joke in this world that brought me as much joy as the word "fartpoop" does to your son." Nadine closes her eyes in embarrassment. "I've told him not to say it in kindergarten," she whispers back, but the teacher shrugs. "I think there isn't a kid in the group who doesn't use their favorite potty word. Kids are all the same in that way." Nadine cautiously pears out through one eye and then opens the second. "Really?" she asks, and her expression brightening. "And here I was thinking that Jack had some kind of feces fixation." Jack's teacher bursts into laughter. "If that were the case, all the kids in kindergarten would probably have it," she says, patting Nadine on the shoulder. "In all seriousness, 'fartpoop' is one of the milder words here."

Jack, who had now put on his jacket, looks at his mom questioningly, putting his hands on his hips. "Mom, why can you say 'fartpoop' and I can't say 'fartpoop'?" he asks. A girl from the group passes by and bursts into loud giggles, shouting, "Fartpoop, fartpoop," so loudly that the parents, who hadn't noticed before, now cast accusing glances at Nadine. Nadine rolls her eyes. "Great," she mutters, looking at her son sternly. "That's why you can't. All the kids would be running around saying it if you said it." Jack's smile, revealing an adorable gap between his teeth, replies, "Well, it would be so much more fun around here."

In the evening, at the dinner table, Nadine tells her husband, Sven, about the incident. She watches as a wide grin spreads across his face, but she quickly redirects his facial muscles with a stern look. "If your mom tells you not to say it to the other kids, then you shouldn't," he says, adopting a serious tone – which now makes Nadine grin a little. Her husband doesn't really suit the role of a strict father. She's convinced he would introduce the "fartpoop" words himself in the kindergarten if he could. He's always been a child at heart, and sometimes Nadine feels she needs to watch over him even more than their son.

"Besides...," Sven starts, reaching for the jar of jam but turning his gaze toward Jack. The jar shatters all over the floor with a loud crash, and Sven jumps up. "Fartpoop!" he shouts loudly, only to immediately cover his mouth with his hand. "I'm sorry," he apologizes to Nadine. "It was the first swear word that came to mind. Definitely, because we were just talking about it." And when Nadine sees her son nearly falling out of his chair with laughter, she suddenly gets an idea.

Seemingly accidentally, she knocks over her empty glass and jumps up. "Bruschetta!" she exclaims and then quickly covers her own mouth with her hand. She looks at her son with widened eyes and begs him, "Forget that word right now." But she has Jack just where she wants him. "What word is that?" he asks, and a grin spreads across his face. Sven, who has already understood his wife's plan, chimes in, "Nadine," he scolds her, "I'm not allowed to say 'fartpoop', but you just said that absolutely forbidden word?" Nadine hides her face in her hands. "What is it?" Jack inquires, but Nadine raises her index finger. "I honestly can't tell you," she says. "Because 'Bruschetta' is not a particularly nice word." And there's one more thing: it really stinks!

A few days later, Nadine is at a parent-teacher meeting. Plans for the coming weeks and the latest updates about the kindergarten are discussed. Like every parent-teacher meeting, this one also seems to drag on endlessly. Nadine has to stifle a yawn as the twentieth mom raises her hand to ask a question that could have been asked in a regular brief conversation. When it's finally over, she quickly grabs her jacket. She thanks the teachers - who have put in a lot of effort to make the evening entertaining - when she hears a mom's voice behind her.

"I absolutely had to ask one more question," she addresses the teacher. "I just can't explain it for the life of me. But for the past few days, my daughter has been running around the house, shouting something about 'bruschetta,' pinching her nose, and laughing like crazy. Can you explain that to me?"

As Nadine leaves the kindergarten, a smile has crept onto her lips. Her plan seems to have worked, and 'fartpoop' finally appears to be a thing of the past.

22. In Different Ways

"You're mollycoddling him too much," Felix comments as he notices the pacifier chain she handmade for him.

"Because of this?" Theresa asks irritably. She'd put so much effort into arranging the woolen threads into a beautiful chain. She made sure not to make it too long to avoid any danger to little Ferdinand, used gender-neutral colors, and incorporated only child-safe decorative elements. She put her heart and soul into making it and felt all the more disappointed when she saw her husband's raised eyebrow.

Still, Felix shakes his head. "A simple chain would have sufficed. Besides, Ferdinand is old enough to reach for his pacifier and pick it up if it falls to the ground." Angrily, Theresa takes the chain and throws it in the trash. "Fine," she mutters to herself. "No pacifier chain."

Then she does what she has done all too often lately. She escapes from the view of her husband and sneaks into her sleeping child. For the past two years, Felix and she have repeatedly clashed over their different parenting styles. Felix believes their son should have as many experiences as possible - even negative ones - to become strong. He thinks Theresa is raising a softy who won't be able to cope without his mom.

Of course, she knows the truth lies somewhere in between. Making a pacifier chain is not the path to happiness, but she has enjoyed making this for her son. While she can't shield Ferdinand from falls and tumbles, the feeling of needing to protect him is overwhelming. Just the thought of Felix being outside somewhere alone with her baby and something happening to him triggers intense panic in her. When Theresa looks at her sleeping boy, she makes a decision and leaves the room as quietly as she came in.

"We really need to talk," she says, looking at her nodding husband. "I agree," he responds, taking a seat at the dining table.

Just as Theresa begins describing how she feels, she sees her son sitting up in bed. Of course, she has a baby monitor that provides both video and room temperature and its reception is always set to high sensitivity. Her husband would've preferred a simple audio baby monitor, but that was out of the question for her. "I'll quickly check on him," Theresa says, but Felix places a hand on her arm. "Wait a moment," he says, pointing to the small screen. As Theresa shakes her head, he holds her arm a bit tighter. "Just a moment. Look, he's perfectly calm. He'll manage to fall asleep again." Theresa gazes at the screen, captivated. And just like that, Ferdinand glances around a few times, then sinks into bed and continues sleeping.

"I am mollycoddling him," Theresa mutters to herself, but the hand resting on her arm now reaches for her hand. "I shouldn't have said that" Felix admits. "It was mean and uncalled for, especially because it's untrue." Theresa looks at Felix questioningly. After all, hadn't it been him telling her that for the past two years, she was being too overprotective? But before she can open her mouth, Felix explains, "It's true that sometimes it's a bit excessive. Ferdinand can hardly explore independently because you're always there to catch him. But I didn't realize you were doing it because you were afraid something might happen to him." Theresa swallows. She really hadn't expected that. "I often think you're way too careless," she admits. "When you're watching over him, Ferdinand gets hurt so often. And I feel that something terrible might happen if I'm not watching." Felix tilts his head. "Really?" he asks, his gaze softening. "Isn't it possible that he gets hurt so often because suddenly he's allowed to try things he otherwise wouldn't, and he overdoes it? Theresa looks at her husband and eventually starts to nod. "I think there might be some truth to that." Felix gives his wife a kiss on the forehead. "And if I pay a bit more attention to your fears, we'll handle it together." Theresa feels something placed in her hand by her husband. When she looks down, she recognizes the beautiful pacifier chain he retrieved from the trash. And she knows her husband is right. Together, they'll make it work.

23. With All the Ups & Downs

"There's no more tissues left, honey," Jana hears her husband's voice as he returns home from work. He sounds a bit sniffly, but that's irrelevant to Jana. The tissues are exactly where they belong after a hard day like today—on her lap and in her hands, ready to dry her tears. "I can't help it," she calls out, trying to make her voice sound firm and confident but failing. Just by the way her husband sticks his head into the room, she can tell that he already knows what's going on.

"Paul or Emil?" he asks as he enters. "Both," Jana groans and leans back into the pillows. "Both turned into real monsters today. And I ran after them like a ranting monster, not liking myself in the process." Jana noisily blows her nose into the last remaining tissue. "You'll have to use toilet paper if you've got a runny nose," she explains to her husband, holding the tissue apologetically. "And bring me some; I'm not done here yet," she says, feeling the next wave of tears coming.

"Are they in bed, or have you banished them to the Monsterland?" Jana's husband, Peter, asks as he enters the bedroom armed with toilet paper, two glasses of wine, and crisps. Jana rolls her eyes. "Yeah, but only after I changed Paul twice because his brother smeared him from head to toe with toothpaste. Oh, and Emil overshot the mark, trying to pee, standing up. After that, I managed to get them into bed. There, they hurled funny swear words at each other, and I did what I'd been doing all day—nagging. And now it's the weekend and tomorrow morning, they'll be delighted to see their daddy again, and everything will be back to normal. The monster costumes will stay in the cupboard, my monster suit can rest for the weekend, and we'll all pretend to be wonderful angels. And on Monday, when you leave the house, everything will be back to normal."

With more force than intended, Jana clinks her glass against Peter's. Red wine splashes onto the bed, and Jana buries her head completely in the pillows. "Great," she sighs and begins to cry again. "The final touch of a terrible day." As Jana and Peter remove the bedsheets and sprinkle vinegar on the red wine stain on the mattress, they hear Paul's voice coming through the baby monitor. "Mommy?"

the little voice calls, and Jana frowns. "Not now," she mutters, hanging her head. Peter places a hand on her shoulder. "I'll go," he says. Shortly after, he hears the bedroom door being opened. "Daddy!" Paul exclaims, and Jana shakes her head. If she didn't know that her children loved her, she might just be jealous of her husband. The man who comes home on the weekend, with whom they can all do fun things, and who rarely experiences the everyday stress.

It doesn't take long before Jana hears her son's whining voice through the speaker. "But I want Mommy," he says, and Jana hears her husband attempting to reassure him. "Mommy is so tired that she's already fallen asleep," Peter invents a little white lie to spare Jana. A small smile spreads across her face. She gets up, leaves the bedroom, goes to the children's room, and quietly opens the door. "Just woke up again," she says, smiling gratefully at her husband. He stands up from the edge of the bed and lets Jana take over. "May I?" she asks, cuddling up under the blanket with her son. She feels him nuzzle his head against her belly and hold her hand. At first, he breathes a bit restlessly. Maybe he just had a bad dream. But then his breathing calms down. Just before he falls asleep, he whispers in his tender child's voice, "I love you, Mommy." He doesn't hear her reply because he has already closed his eyes.

And Jana realizes once again that she can overcome any deep pit. She'll transform into the scolding monster a few more times, and her sons will often put on the monster costumes they had on today. But that's perfectly fine because every tear is worth shedding when there are moments like this one where they can sit together so united.

24. The Ability to Cast a Spell

"Honestly, Mom, this is so embarrassing," Hanna groans as she watches her mom stomp through the house. She looks like a big, physically impaired stork in a salad as she searches for Hanna's little sister, Tessa. She turns her head exaggeratedly in all directions as if it were on a rubbery neck, unable to decide which way to look. "Where's my little Tessi mouse?" Hanna's mom calls out loudly throughout the living room. Hanna glances at three-year-old Tessa, who peeks out from under the sofa and stifles a giggle by covering her mouth with her hand. With a loud "THERE YOU AREEEEEE," Hanna's mom snatches up the little girl and spins her around, laughing. "I found you," she exclaims, blowing raspberries on the youngest family member's belly.

"You really don't have to go over the top like that all the time," Hanna says, rolling her eyes, even though she can see how much fun her little sister is having with the hide-and-seek game. "And besides, Mom always knows where you are, Tessa." The little girl looks at her mom, puzzled, but she shakes her head. "That's what your big sister thinks," she explains. "When you're as old as she is, you don't have any fun at all. Then you have to run around like a grumpy monster." Her mom pulls her eyelids down just a bit, sticks her tongue out, and makes strange noises. Hanna rolls her eyes. The eleven-year-old girl can't understand for the life of her how her mom can be so silly. When she started school, she had gotten out of the habit of playing children's games; she was finally a big girl. Now, in high school, she wouldn't dream of having an imaginary tea party with her little sister and pretending that there was something other than air in the plastic cups. Nor would she stir an empty saucepan only to bring an empty spoon to her mouth and pretend how delicious the fine soup was. And she definitely wouldn't stomp around the living room like a stork in a salad pretending to look for the girl who was actually right in front of her eyes.

"I'm going outside; it's too silly in here," Hanna says, gathering her things and dashing into the garden. There, she sits on the swing. Instead of swinging like young children, she casually props her leg up and looks around. She leans against the swing's rope at her back, hoping her school friends can see her. She is convinced that she looks pretty cool.

"Mom, really? I said I wanted to be left alone," Hanna grumbles as her mom brings Tessa outside. "I don't need you to be fooling around out here too." But the mom winks at her daughter. "Don't worry," she says. "I have to cook dinner. And because I have such a caring, older daughter, you can watch the little one for a moment." Without waiting for a response, Hanna rolls her eyes as her mom enters without waiting for a reply. Of course, she knows the property is entirely secured, so not much can actually happen to Tessa, but still, she's definitely not the babysitter here.

The mom stands in the kitchen, peeking through the curtains. She lovingly watches her two daughters - the little one, who is happily running around the garden, and the older one, who keeps throwing her hair back and adjusting her sitting position to look a little cooler. "What a challenging time it was when I had to prove that I no longer belonged with the little ones," the mom thinks to herself as she stirs in a saucepan which, for once, had something inside it. As she tastes the sauce, she looks up and sees her little one fall flat on her face after tripping up while running. A few seconds later, Tessa sits up and yells loudly. Just as she is about to turn off the stove and rush outside to her, she notices Hanna jump off the swing and run towards her little sister, helping her back on her feet and checking her hands. And then, when her youngest still doesn't stop crying, Hanna blows on Tessa's hands. She points into the air and waves goodbye to the flying.

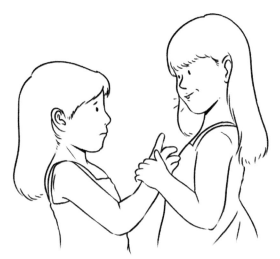

'Ouch'. The mom watches with a smile – because it's truly reassuring to know that her cool daughter still can wave an imaginary 'ouch' to comfort her little sister.

25. A Cuppa Tea

"Madam, may I have this pleasure?" Thea asks her daughter Lisa while pulling the chair back. Affectionately, she sets the table with the fine tea set she gifted her daughter on her second birthday. "Would you like a little cup of tea?" she asks, and Lea claps her hands excitedly. Lisa takes one of the small cups, goes to the kitchen, pours some water, comes back, and places it on the table. The little girl brings the cup up to her mouth and is about to drink when Lisa says, "Careful, you need to blow; it's hot." Together, they blow into the cup.

"Oops," says Lea, and Lisa gets up from the table to fetch a kitchen towel. "Don't worry, it's no big deal," she explains and dries the water that landed on the table. "It can happen to anyone." Lisa winks at her daughter, and the game continues.

"Lea wants more tea." the girl suggests, and Lisa nods. But as she gets up, the girl shakes her head. "Lea, do it alone," she explains. Lisa raises her index finger.

"One moment," she says, getting up from the little tea table. "I'll prepare everything. Otherwise, you won't be able to." Lisa rushes to the kitchen and places a small stool in front of the sink. Since the water already has a temperature limit, she has no qualms about leaving her daughter alone at the tap.

"Done," she says, smiling at her daughter. "Now you can make a tea." Lea happily jumps off the table, grabs the two teacups, and runs out of the room.

"On the way back, you need to go slower," Lisa calls after her daughter. "Otherwise, it might spill."

Naturally, this warning doesn't help too much. When Lea returns with the teacups, she leaves a trail of water drops behind her. "Lea is spilling," the girl laughs, but Lisa waves it off. "We can clean it up later," she says. "For now, let's play." Lisa is delighted that her daughter has taken a liking to this little task. Again and again, the child runs off to fetch water.

"Thank you very much," the mom plays, knowing that constant repetition tends to be more memorable for toddlers. "Oops," Lisa says as she sees the contents of her teacup spilling over the table. "Lea goes," the child says and returns shortly with a few sheets of toilet paper. "Well, you could have got some kitchen paper," Lisa laughs, wiping the table. "Lea can't reach it," the girl explains, but Lisa looks at her, shaking her head. "It's right next to the sink," she explains. "You just needed to pull on the paper, and you would have been able to reach it. But it's not a big deal. Toilet paper soaks up our tea just as well."

"Now, your turn again," the girl says after a while, holding out the teacups to her mom. Lisa stands up and announces, "But this is the last tea. Otherwise, I might turn into a teacup later." She hears her daughter's laughter behind her as she hops over all the spilled water. She avoids the first puddle, jumps over the second, and steps right into the third.

"Oh well," she says with a shrug. Her socks are already wet, so she no longer focuses on the water trail.

Once Lisa arrives in the kitchen, she looks around in surprise. The stool she'd placed for her daughter is gone. "Lea? How did you reach the water?" she asks aloud, hearing her daughter's voice from the living room. "Stool," she calls, but Lisa still can't see the stool. Looking down at the floor, she is surprised that the water trail has also disappeared. Lisa returns to the hallway and follows the trail, which leads in a different, unexpected direction.

"Oh no," Lisa mutters as she recognizes the path the water trail on the floor takes. She can hardly bring herself to look into the bathroom, but that's precisely where the trail leads. She sends up a silent prayer, hoping so much that the stool will be placed in front of the sink in the bathroom – but unfortunately, her prayer goes unanswered as she finds the stool exactly where she had hoped not to find it.

26. Rotated Several Times

"Would you mind telling me how many times you plan to rotate this note before you plan to give it to the shop assistant?" Amelie hears her friend's voice. Startled, she looks up. "Sorry, I didn't even realize was it my turn," she stammers and hands the twenty euro note to the waiting shop assistant. The woman continues to wait, and Amelie glances at the cash register. "Oh my," she mutters, feeling herself blush. It's just a few cents more.

This time, Amelie must have been really not paying attention. She usually calculates down to the cent when she has
to stop adding items to her shopping basket. "I don't have
any more cash with me," she says. The cashier looks at
Amelie skeptically. "With a card?" she asks, but Amelie
shakes her head. "My husband has it," she laughs to cover
up the awkward situation. Amelie's friend is close to intervening when the young mom holds her back. She knows
full well that Erika wants to give her the money, but it's not
what she wants. "Can you please take off the granola bar?"
she asks and sees the cashier briefly roll her eyes. She feels
her cheeks blush even more, and for a moment, she closes
her eyes.

"And what are you going to eat now?" asks Amelie's friend
after they leave the store. "Oh," Amelie says and waves it
off. "I'm not really hungry." In reality, she wanted to buy
the granola bar because she felt like she was going to pass
out from low blood sugar. The banana she'd brought from
home was so brown when she opened it that there was no
way she could eat it. "I can wait until I get home; I'm sure
my husband has already cooked," Amelie laughs at her
friend - knowing that there isn't much left in the fridge at

home from which they could cook anything. After all, it's the end of the month, and money is already tight. "Have I told you that we're going on vacation?" Amelie asks, quickly changing the subject from this uncomfortable topic.

"Yes?" Amelie's friend asks, and without thinking, she blurts out, "We booked a vacation yesterday too. Three weeks in the Caribbean, all-inclusive, it's going to be amazing." She stops herself in her excitement with an apologetic look, saying, "I'm sorry!" Of course, she knows that Amelie can only dream of such a vacation – even though she doesn't know just how dire Amelie's financial situation actually is.

"We're planning to go to the Baltic Sea," Amelie says, forcing a smile. But her friend looks at her with a questioning expression. "Be honest," she says unexpectedly. "How often do you have to go without a granola bar to afford this?" Amelie wants to backtrack, as she always does, when the unexpected topic of 'money' comes up, but this time, her friend won't let her get away with it. "I don't want you to feel ashamed," she says. "But this can't go on. You've been hardly eating anything for days, and I'm sure there's no hot meal waiting for you. You've sewn a patch on your trousers, although they're already worn everywhere. You cut your hair yourself and have all these excuses when I ask if we should go out for breakfast. I'm not dumb. I know you've been struggling to make ends meet since Jonas was born. Your salary has decreased because you no longer get tips, and your expenses have increased. Do you really think taking Jonas on a vacation is the only way to make him happy? Or can you buy that granola bar and a new pair of pants, save the extra money, and he'll be just as happy? That way, you can even afford a nice paddling pool for the garden - and a pair of trunks for Jonas, too."

Tears well up in Amelie's eyes. She and her husband had tried so hard to afford a vacation. She didn't want her son to go without anything. "Amelie," her friend says, hugging her, "Jonas has everything he needs. He has the two best parents imaginable, and whether he spends time with you in the paddling pool at home or the Baltic Sea, he doesn't care – as long as you're with him."

Amelie wipes away her tears when she breaks free from her friend's embrace. She retrieves the emergency cash from her purse, which she had been determined not to touch, and heads back into the store she'd just left. It's about time she bought a granola bar.

27. A Change of Scenery

"What happened here?" Torben asks when he comes home. He notices that the place that had been his home until this morning looks completely different.

"I desperately needed a change of scenery," mumbles Bettina, with a paintbrush clenched between her teeth, standing precariously atop a wobbly ladder. The subtle beige wall color of the living room has given way to a vibrant orange, the furniture is arranged entirely differently than it was in the morning – some pieces are entirely missing – and the television has also completely disappeared.

"A change of scenery," Tjorben states soberly, looking skeptically around the new living room. "Do you think you've achieved what you wanted?" With a loud "Uhhhh," Bettina jumps off the ladder into her husband's arms. She surveys the room and nods. "I have," she says, tossing the paintbrush into the paint can, splattering a bright orange spot on the trash bag spread out below. "Don't you like it?" she asks, looking at her doubting husband.

"Well," he says, looking around the room once more. He cautiously asks, "Don't you think the orange might be a tad too bright for us?" But Bettina shakes her head. "Absolutely not," she says, glancing at the baby monitor to check if their son was still peacefully sleeping in his room.

"I thought we desperately needed a change. Everything was becoming so worn out, and I was withering away in that dreary beige," Tjorben nods as he hears his wife's words. "And it wouldn't have been enough to order pizza tonight, even though it's supposed to be a vegetable day?" he asks, receiving a hearty shoulder shove from his wife. "We have vegetables – like every Tuesday," she says, hearing her husband's muffled voice, "I suspected as much."

While Tjorben takes off his jacket and shoes, Bettina reheats dinner. "Derek finally tried carrots," she tells her husband. "But he found them disgusting."

But Tjorben is currently more interested in a different topic than his son's lack of awareness that vegetables are good for him. "What did you have in mind for tonight?" he asks cautiously. Bettina grins at him. "You mean because

I've banished the TV?" Tjorben nods uncertainly. His wife's grin doesn't bode well.

"I was thinking," she begins and grins even wider, "we should go without that old thing for a while. Sometimes, we're glued to it in the evenings. For tonight, I've picked out some games for us, and in the coming days, we could listen to music together, talk, read a book, or do other things." Bettina winks flirtatiously at her husband, who now finds the idea of banishing the TV not so bad after all – if you leave out the music, the book, or the games.

"The orange looks like shit!" Bettina lies in her husband's arms, looking around. "And the games are boring." She feels her husband nod against the back of her head. "And right now, the movie I was looking forward to last week is on," he adds to the list of unpleasant things his wife had just initiated.

"Orange," she repeats and covers her eyes. "How could I ever think that orange would fit in our living room?" She hears Tjorben's soft voice: "You needed a change of scenery not to wither away in that drab beige," he roughly recalls the words she had said to him earlier. Bettina shakes her head doubtfully. "But couldn't a pizza have sufficed? On vegetable day?" she now asks in turn and peeks cautiously behind her hands that she had used to cover her eyes. "It doesn't get any better the more you look at it," she observes with a laugh. "And I'm bored. Let's get the TV."

Tjorben doesn't need to be told a second time. He quickly jumps up from the sofa and rushes to the storage room. A short while later, he presses the button on the remote control. "But don't fall asleep," he tells his wife, who often dozes off in front of the TV. "The movie is supposed to be extremely thrilling."

When Bettina is still awake during the ad break, Tjorben nudges her and says, "What do you think about us going to the Baltic Sea tomorrow and staying there over the weekend?" Bettina is about to protest, but Tjorben continues. "You said you needed a change of scenery. And before you turn our house into a teepee next week, I'd like to change things up."

Bettina nods and looks again at the ugly wall color. She knows that a change has been missing in her life lately. And a short break from the daily routine is just what she needs right now.

28. Ornithologist

Eight-year-old Betti grabs her little beginner's camera. For the first time in her life, a pair of birds have built a nest right outside her window. As Betti holds the camera to her eyes, closes one eye, looks through the camera, and adjusts the settings to maximum magnification, she can see a blackbird and thrush flying back and forth to build the perfect nest. They're working to create a little, perfect home for their little ones who will soon arrive.

Fifteen-year-old Betti kneels on the floor. She can see the bird's nest safely nestled between the trees from this angle. She sets her new camera to automatic mode, attaches the lens, and zooms in as closely as possible. Carefully, she creeps closer to the nest, watches, assesses, and shoots one photo after another. The thrush sits in the middle of the nest, looking around attentively, protecting what is growing beneath her warm body.

Twenty-two-year-old Betti finally pulls out her camera after a long time. She walks slowly to the shed, making sure not to disturb the birds. She crouches in a corner, correctly adjusting the settings following the exposure triangle. After all, the photos must be perfect. With the camera raised, she peers through the viewfinder, remaining completely still. Every time the bird's parents fly into the nest, she takes a series of shots. For brief moments, the bird babies peek out of the nest, open their beaks, and feed on what their parents offer them, trusting in their protection.

Twenty-seven-year-old Betti sits in her camouflage tent in the garden, patiently waiting for the thrush and the fledgling bird babies to come close enough so she can capture the moment with her camera. She takes one photo after another. They are photos showing how the baby birds have left the safety of their nest, knowing their parents are there to continue feeding and protecting them. The 32-year-old Betti looks into the camera, not used to behind the one in front of the lens. Her usual position is behind - but not today. Today, her husband is taking photos of her. She's decorating the room, painting the walls, and setting up a baby crib. She wants to create a little, perfect home for her little one who'll soon arrive.

32-year-old Betti hears the camera focusing and clicking as it takes a photo. She sits in an armchair, wrapped in a warm blanket. Her arms rest on her belly, protecting what is growing inside her warm body.

The 32-year-old Betti sees the flash, set to its dimmest level, as her husband takes a photo. She sits in a rocking chair in the baby's room, holding her baby protectively under a blanket while she feeds. The baby completely trusts in being protected.

41-year-old Betti hears the camera's frantic shutter release, representing hundreds of pictures taken within seconds. She laughs into the camera as she watches her daughter go wild with her new toy. Not a single picture will be sharp, but that's okay. After all, Betti is right here, watching over the little girl, helping her learn new things, protecting her for as long as she lives.

80-year-old Betti hands her daughter a photo album. It's an album of various blackbirds and thrushes that Betti has been photographing her life. It's an album that shows how life continues to progress. It's an album in which Betti is also seen preparing a room, providing a home for a baby, protecting a baby, and assisting a girl as she grows up. It's an album that reveals to a woman who has now grown up how life comes from life and what love and security look like. It's a reminder of a time when Betti won't be there anymore to protect her.

Betti takes her camera, turns it around, rests her head against her daughter's, and takes a photo. The pictures are no longer as sharp as they used to be, blurred by the old woman's trembling hands. Yet, it's a photo that will mean a lot to one grown-up woman someday—a memory of mother and daughter.

29. Matrimonial

"Honey, did you wash my shirt?" Frank shouts so loudly through the house that Emma, who was standing right behind him, nearly has her ears blown off. But of course," she yells back and sees her husband flinch. "Why are you yelling like that?" he asks accusingly, and Emma responds with a counter-question. "I don't know. Why are you yelling like that?" Then, she takes the freshly washed baby clothes out of the dryer.

When Emma sees her husband struggling to tie a tie, she bursts into laughter. "Sorry," she says when she notices her husband's raised eyebrow. "May I?" Her hands quickly tie the perfect knot, neat and elegant. "Thank you, honey," her husband says, kissing her on the forehead just before he heads off to work. Emma still had to dress the baby, who was lying cozily in a sleeping bag in front of her.

"No, it's far too cold. You should definitely put on a jacket." Emma remarks as she sees her husband, in just his shirt, about to leave the house. She stops him at the last moment. "I know the sun is shining," she says when she sees him about to protest. "But it's only three degrees, and it's too cold to go outside without a jacket." Emma presses the jacket into his hands, gives him a kiss, and sends him off to work. Then, she wraps her baby in a warm jacket, puts a hat on him, and sets off for a morning walk.

Emma is just about to tackle the tasks that must be done at her home office for the day; not a single word has been typed when her phone rings. "I just needed to hear your voice," her husband says, "I miss you and would much rather be with you right now." Emma exchanges a few words with her husband and says her goodbyes, explaining that she needs to get back to work before the baby wakes up. As she ends the call, she hears her baby starting to cry through the baby monitor. She gets up and retrieves the little one from the crib. She speaks soothingly, knowing that he wants to be with her.

Shortly before 6:00 PM, Emma prepares dinner. She has spent the entire day tending to her small baby, taking him for walks, holding and rocking him after its midday nap, and still managing to complete some writing tasks. Now, she looks forward to her husband's coming home and having dinner together. "I'm home," her husband's voice echoes from the hallway. Emma places the steaming plates on the table, taking her time to eat with her husband. A few drops of hot soup run down his chin, and Emma quickly grabs a cloth to wipe the stain from his shirt. She fetches her baby from the nursery, sits in the nursing chair, and feeds him before wiping the spilled milk from his chin.

At night, long after Emma and her husband have gone to sleep, she hears a sound from the nursery. The baby has woken up. As if in a trance, she gets up, sways into the dimly lit room, lifts him up, gently rocking him in her arms, singing a lullaby. When he finally falls back asleep, Emma heads back to the bedroom. She then takes her husband's head, cradles it gently in her arms, and sings him a lullaby. He looks at her with doubt and will never fully be able to understand that, as a mom and wife, she is accustomed to doing every task twice.

30. In the Name of Love

Julia holds her crying child in her arms. "I wish," sobs the nine-year-old girl, "I wish I had a normal family." Julia's breath catches. It had never crossed her mind that her daughter could perceive their family as not normal. She gently pushes her child away to look into her eyes more closely. "Do you believe we're not a normal family, Nele?" she asks, and the girl shakes her head, nods, and then shakes her head again.

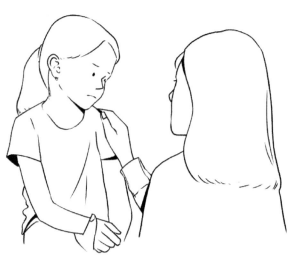

"We learned today what a normal family is, and we're very different," Nele explains. Julia is taken aback. She knew a family project was happening at school all week, but she didn't expect Nele to be critical of their family. "And what IS a normal family?" Julia inquires, with a very concrete picture in mind.

"Well," the girl says, shrugging her shoulders. "It's when a mom and a dad have a child. And then they wanted us to draw our family, but I couldn't draw my mom and dad." Julia gazes into her daughter's eyes. "You couldn't?" she asks. "Do you want me to give you a picture of Dad and me? Then you can glue it or trace it." Nele rolls her eyes and says, "You know exactly what I mean." But Julia persists. "I always thought," she says, "that we are your parents." Nele gets really angry. "But you didn't give BIRTH to me!" she says. "A real family is only when a mom and a dad GIVE BIRTH to a child!"

Julia breathes a sigh of relief. Her daughter has finally expressed what must have been going through her head in recent days. "You know," she explains, putting her arm around the girl she and her husband adopted shortly after birth, "Lisa in your class has two moms, right?" Nele nods. "So, does Lisa not have a real family?" Nele shakes her head. "No, she does. One of her mommies gave birth to her," she says. But Julia interjects, "But the other mom didn't give birth to her." She continues, "Felix lives with his mom, but his dad lives far away because his parents got divorced." "Are they not a real family because of that?" Nele covers her eyes with her hands. "Oh, Mom, you don't understand," she says. "Of course, they're a real family because Felix's mom and dad are his real mom and dad."

Julia gently lowers her daughter's hands. "I understand what you want to say," she explains. "But I don't agree with you. Daddy and I adopted you when you were just a baby." Julia takes out her phone and opens the gallery, displaying pictures of Nele as a baby. "We changed your nappies." She shows her daughter a photo where she put a clean diaper over Nele's head because she'd forgotten her hat on a cold walk. "We took care of all your cuts and bruises." Next, she shows the picture of Nele with a bandage around her head because she fell from a tree. "We fed you." Now, they look at the photo where Nele is eating her first baby food. Her face is smeared red, and she proudly smiles at the camera with a spoon in her hand. "We watched you learn new things." Now, the photos show Nele riding a bike for the first time and holding up her swimming badge. Julia lowers her phone.

"Dad and I have carried you, protected you, rocked you to sleep, and we've been there for everything you've learned up until now. We've done the tasks that a mom and dad have as well as we could. We've made some mistakes along the way, but when I look at you like this, we did a lot right, too. There are no normal or abnormal families. Every family is entirely different from the others. You may not have grown in my belly in our family, but you've grown in Daddy's and my heart. And that's what matters - love is what makes a family.

A Few Final Words

Together with the moms from the last 30 stories, you've experienced highs and lows and, hopefully, shared a few chuckles and been touched by them. They're all moms like you and me, who, on some days, are teetering on the brink of insanity and, on other days, are pulled back by their children's love.

I must admit that as a mother, I've experienced some of the stories described myself – not only joining an unintentional anti-lesbian demonstration on the street (and I'm certainly open to any relationship constellation) but also telling my own daughter that I was getting a new tattoo, to which she asked if it would be colorful. After explaining to her that I was only getting the lines done that day, she shouted across the school carpark that I was going to get "lines" that day.

You yourself surely have experienced familiar situations where no explanation seems to help. And if your child is still too young to have embarrassed you so far, you can look forward to it because no mom escapes being exposed by their own children.

Fortunately, I wasn't given tea water from the toilet by my child but instead was privileged to describe this situation to you.

10 minutes of downtime each day. If you've managed it as planned, you've been through the last 30 days and should not give it up. These 10 minutes are for you. They're meant for you to recharge so you can continue to be the super-mom you really are, with all the ups and downs and justified mood swings.

Keep taking short breaks that make you feel good. Take the time to do something just for you because you're worth it. You are what your child needs:

A supermom without a cape!

Thank You So Much

We hope you enjoyed the book. If you have any questions, suggestions or feedback, please feel free to email us at Info@siimpo.de.

We're an up-and-coming small publishing house with a passion for entertaining all members of the family providing inspiration and ease in everyday life. Our precisely crafted and thoughtful guides aim to make life a little easier. If you appreciate our work and would like to support us, we look forward to your review on Amazon.

Simply follow the link https://amzn.to/413tl0K or scan this QR code:

Liability

This book contains the opinions and ideas of the author and is intended to provide helpful and informative knowledge to people. The strategies included may not be suitable for every reader, and there is no guarantee that they will work for everyone. The use of this book and the implementation of the information contained therein are expressly at your own risk.

Claims for damages, whether of a material or immaterial nature, resulting from the use or non-use of the information or from the use of incorrect and/or incomplete information, are expressly excluded. The work, including all its contents, provides no warranty or guarantee for the timeliness, correctness, completeness, and quality of the information provided. Printing errors and misinformation cannot be completely ruled out.

Imprint

Unabridged Edition 2023 – 1st Edition: September 2023

ISBN: 9798868068287

© 2023 Verena Schuster – Information according to §5 TMG

The author is represented by:

Marklet, Jessica Scollo,

Vogesenstr. 14a, DE,

Info@siimpo.de,

2186904787

VAT ID: DE343186079

Stock Images: Depositphotos.com

Illustrations: Raihan Muhammad

Printing: Amazon and Partner

Printed in Great Britain
by Amazon

37190174R00088